TULSA CITY-COUNTY LIB

D1193428

From Home to School Literacy 1&2

Stories and Activities for Parents

Teacher's Guide

Ann Gianola
Instructor, San Diego Community College District
San Diego, California

New Readers Press

TULSA CITY-COUNTY LIB

Thank you to Ann Marie Damrau, San Diego Community College District, for
help and advice in the development of the literacy level of *From Home to School.*

From Home to School Teacher's Guide
ISBN 978-1-56420-491-2

Copyright © 2004 New Readers Press
New Readers Press
Division of ProLiteracy Worldwide
1320 Jamesville Avenue, Syracuse, New York 13210
www.newreaderspress.com

All rights reserved. No part of this book may be reproduced or transmitted in any form or
by any means, electronic or mechanical, including photocopying, recording, or by any
information storage and retrieval system, without permission in writing from the publisher.

Printed in the United States of America
9   8   7   6   5   4

All proceeds from the sale of New Readers Press materials
support literacy programs in the United States and worldwide.

Acquisitions Editor: Paula L. Schlusberg
Content Editor: Terrie Lipke
Production Manager: Andrea Woodbury
Designer: Kimbrly Koennecke
Production Specialist: Jeffrey R. Smith
Cover Design: Kimbrly Koennecke

Contents

Level 2 Lesson Notes 31

Overview

From Home to School is a three-level set of materials that provides stories and activities specifically designed for adult learners in family literacy programs or in ABE or adult ESL classes. The student books are intended both for native speakers with limited reading skills and for English language learners at literacy, low-beginning, and high-beginning levels. *From Home to School 1* and *2* each have an accompanying workbook focused on language skills. The workbooks are intended primarily for ESL learners but may be suitable for others as well. In *From Home to School Literacy,* stories from levels 1 and 2 have been simplified to meet the needs of literacy-level and very-low-proficiency students.

The goal of *From Home to School* is to raise issues of importance to parents of elementary-school-age children and to provide opportunities for discussion, critical thinking, and problem-solving. Lessons are based on relevant but entertaining readings about common concerns parents have about school. They include interactions between parents and school personnel and between parents and children regarding school matters. Because the readings highlight topics they can relate to, students are motivated to develop reading fluency while becoming more familiar with school-related issues. Follow-up activities lead to further exploration and better understanding of the issues, while also building vocabulary and practical communication skills. The teaching and learning strategies in these exercises may also be helpful to parents at home, giving them confidence to assume more active roles in their children's education.

With focused lessons, even at the literacy level, students learn to understand the U.S. school system better. They also develop confidence in their ability to speak and act effectively and appropriately when faced with common school-related situations (e.g., responding to information about a child's health, reporting a bully at school, receiving a phone call from the teacher, etc.). The stories provide opportunities for students to learn about school procedures and expectations, to explore their own values and ways of interacting with their children, to share ideas and solutions, and to learn appropriate ways to express themselves when dealing with similar situations.

The 15 stories in each student book portray diverse characters in interesting and often challenging situations. In level 1, students are introduced to Mrs. Yong, who volunteers in her daughter's classroom. They meet Max, who is upset by a bully at school. Readers also get to know Jamal and his mother, who have a difference of opinion at a shoe store; Willie, who is too sick to go to school; and several others. In level 2, students meet Alain, who is frequently late for school. They get to know Roza, who does not understand her daughter's report card. Readers are also introduced to Pavel and his father, who use flash cards to practice multiplication; Justine, who talks too much in class; and others with whom students can identify. The adapted stories at the literacy level introduce students to selected characters from the other two levels.

Lesson themes in *From Home to School 1* and *2* parallel each other, although specific topics are different at each level. For example, the health-themed lesson in level 2 deals with head lice, while the same lesson in level 1 deals with routine vision screening. At the literacy level, stories parallel selected stories from either level 1 or 2. Having level-appropriate stories with parallel themes provides continuity for students moving from one level to another. Also, two or all three levels can be used simultaneously with a multilevel group, allowing students to work at different levels but share information and ideas about related topics.

Audio recordings for levels 1 and 2 provide a reading of each story, the dialog for each lesson, and prompts for all listening activities. They also include prompts for workbook listening activities. There is no audio recording for the literacy level, but optional listening activities, with directions for teachers, appear at the end of the student book.

From Home to School can be used independently or as a supplement to any core curriculum. The stories tie into general ESL themes and deal with issues related to commonly taught life-skills topics such as food, shopping, health, and daily routines.

The lessons in *From Home to School* are not designed to be sequential, so the stories can be taught in any order. At the literacy level, however, the stories increase very slightly in difficulty through the latter part of the book. If the stories are read in order, students can progress toward slightly higher proficiency levels by building upon skills practiced in earlier lessons.

Using *From Home to School Literacy*

The 15 stories selected for adaptation to the literacy level contain important messages that can be clearly understood by students at this stage of language development. Each lesson includes practice in manageable amounts of reading, writing, listening, and speaking. Predictable, simple follow-up exercises lead to level-appropriate exploration of issues and better understanding of school practices while building vocabulary and practical communication skills.

The lessons are designed to build language skills as students progress through activities. The reading presents a story in clear language, with each sentence or pair of short sentences on a single line. Following each reading, a cloze exercise (*Complete the story.*) reproduces the story in paragraph form, to reinforce the content and vocabulary. Following this, there is a comprehension-checking activity (*Check yes or no.*), an exercise where the issues are related directly to the student (*Check yes or no about you.*), a concise dialog so that students can practice routine interactions, and concluding exercises that reinforce the key point of the story and assess students' understanding of the language and main issues.

Each story opens with an illustration. A second illustration appears at the end of the story. For literacy-level learners, using words to identify objects in pictures is an important first step in vocabulary building. Illustrations are effective tools for introducing stories because they create interest and help students to reflect on previous experiences. Pictures are also useful for preteaching vocabulary, practicing pronunciation, and even predicting events and outcomes.

The illustrations should have a major role at this level. Encourage students to carefully examine the pictures. They contain context clues that will facilitate general comprehension, drawing conclusions, or reading for specific information. Teach or review the names of items or actions students see, or prompt students to name them by asking questions. Consider expanding each lesson with additional pictures from magazines or newspapers, clip art images, and pictures drawn by students (e.g., clock, school bus, stop sign).

Whenever possible, it is helpful to show real items that are mentioned in a story. Collect or have students bring in various items from their children's schools: health notices, cafeteria menus, parent-teacher conference schedules, report cards, memos from the office, and other things applicable to lessons.

Graphic organizers can provide effective tools for either preview or follow-up. A KWL chart, for example, can be used to elicit and record what students already know about a topic or issue, what they want to know, and then, after they complete a lesson, what they have learned from the reading and activities.

What I Already Know	What I Want to Know	What I Have Learned

Consider using the story title to encourage predictions and elicit prior experiences. Also look at the speech bubbles that were added to many of the illustrations in this level. Speech bubbles clarify who is speaking and what message the character wishes to convey. Try labeling pictures with additional phrases. This can lead to the creation of simple exchanges or dialogs as in a comic strip. Language generated from students may or may not relate directly to the actual story. Still, this can be an excellent way to engage a student who is not ready to decode longer passages.

Before reading a story, consider listing new words on cards or on the board. Introduce synonyms or antonyms to build vocabulary. Put words into categories (e.g., family members, sports, things in the classroom, etc.) and elicit other examples. Also try dividing words into groups depending on pronunciation or spelling (e.g., words that contain the *i* vowel sound in *is* or words that end in the letter *e*).

To present the stories, you may prefer to have students first just listen to the stories, or listen and follow the written text, while you model pronunciation and structure. Emphasizing sentence structure helps students create their own sentences in English. Pose a general comprehension question to focus students' listening (and reading). On repetitions of the story, you may want to add more specific questions.

Begin also to introduce the conventions of written English. Point out capital letters and periods, quotation marks for direct speech, and indents at the beginnings of paragraphs (as in the cloze exercise).

Use the cloze exercise *(Complete the story.)* to integrate the four language skills: reading, writing, listening, and speaking. This activity presents the story in paragraph form. It requires students to refer to the story to find specific words and see where the words fit into sentences. Students also get additional reading practice. After students complete the cloze exercise, have them listen to sentence starters and complete the sentences orally to reconstruct lines from the story.

A comprehension-checking activity *(Check yes or no.)* follows each cloze story. This exercise should first be done orally at this level. Then students can follow along and check their answers as you read. Encourage students to refer back to the story for details they may not remember. If an answer is *no,* have students provide a correct restatement if possible. This exercise may be done very slowly, focusing on speaking before writing. To follow up, have students retell pieces of the story in their own words, either individually or with a partner. You can also write down what students say, creating another version of the story for additional reading practice.

The next exercise *(Check yes or no about you.)* isolates details or key messages from the story and relates them directly to the student. For example, when the main character in a story is from Mexico, the student must check *yes* or *no* to "I am from

Mexico." Again, if the answer is *no,* help students to make correct statements, either positive (e.g., "I am from China.") or negative (e.g., "I am not from Mexico.").

Each lesson contains a dialog based directly on the story or on a related situation (e.g., what a parent can say to school personnel regarding a child's situation or problem as presented in the story). The purpose of the dialog at this level is to model what might be said in an effective conversation. Have students listen before reading the dialog. Model it several times if necessary. Check comprehension and discuss content. Model the dialog again, stopping after each line to allow students to repeat what was said. This activity prepares students to act it out themselves and provides useful pronunciation practice. Students can then practice with partners, creating role-plays featuring parents, teachers, and other school personnel.

Adapting dialogs to fit student needs is especially useful. Indicate to students that there may be more than one way to say the same thing, and teach or review other phrases with similar meanings. Also highlight key phrases in dialogs that can be used in other contexts. For example, you must identify your child when you call the school office—no matter what the reason (e.g., reporting absence, tardiness, medical appointments, etc.). Many dialogs are also followed by short-answer comprehension questions to check understanding.

A concluding activity (e.g., *Complete the sentences.*) assesses whether students have understood the main point and tests recognition and correct usage of words in the story. Other culminating activities include matching useful words or phrases with pictures. This requires students to make distinctions between scenes or items and to label them correctly.

For additional oral practice, listening exercise prompts and directions are included at the end of the book. These oral exercises reinforce key vocabulary and phrases from the stories and allow students to practice transcribing times, days, numbers, etc.

To begin the listening exercises, have students number lines on a sheet of paper. Then read the directions aloud. Read each prompt, and give students time to write the answers. At this level, you may need to read each prompt twice before students write. If necessary, repeat the prompt a third time after students have completed writing. Check answers by having volunteers write their answers on the board.

Using *From Home to School 1* and *2*

Each story opens with two prereading questions and an illustration. Another illustration appears on the second page of the story. These provide effective tools for introducing a story. You can begin with either the questions or the illustrations.

In warm-up or preview activities, the illustrations can help create interest in the story, provide a starting point for discussion, and help introduce new vocabulary. Have students look at the illustrations, particularly the one that precedes the story. Encourage students to describe what they see, or prompt them with questions (e.g., "What do you see? Where are these people? What is he/she doing? Is he happy? Why or why not?"). If possible, have students use the illustration to guess what the story is about or to predict the story's outcome. Keep in mind that students' responses may vary at this level. Some students may express themselves fluently, while others may be limited to simple phrases or even single words.

Another effective way to introduce a story is with the two prereading questions. Use those questions to stimulate discussion, and to encourage students to share pertinent information about their lives at home and their children's experiences at school. The questions can form the basis for whole-class or small-group discussions on such topics as bedtime, extracurricular activities, and homework.

Graphic organizers of various types are effective tools for either preview or follow up. As previously noted (p. 6), a KWL chart can be used to elicit and record what students already know about a topic or issue, what they want to know, and then, after they complete a lesson, what they have learned from the reading and activities.

An interview grid can stimulate discussion or help learners organize information about schools.

Student	Question 1	Question 2	Question 3
A	Answer	Answer	Answer
B	Answer	Answer	Answer

Whenever possible, show real items that pertain to a story when discussing school issues. Collect or have students bring in various papers from school: health notices, cafeteria menus, parent-teacher conference schedules, report cards, memos from the office, and other documents related to lesson topics.

To present the stories, you can have students first listen to the audio recording one or more times to get a sense of the story line. Or you may prefer to have students initially follow the written text while listening to the recording. Pose a general comprehension question to focus students' listening (and reading). On repetitions of the story, you may want to add other, more specific questions.

In level 1, a comprehension exercise (*Check Yes or No.*) follows each story. If an answer is *no*, have students provide a correct restatement. In level 2, a comprehension exercise (*Answer the Questions.*) follows each story. Encourage students to respond to questions using complete sentences. These activities can be done orally or in writing. As a follow-up, have students retell the story in their own words, either individually or in groups. You can also write down what students say, creating another version of the story for additional reading practice.

Vocabulary exercises follow the comprehension checks in each lesson. These exercises reinforce students' understanding of words from the story and expand their vocabulary with related words. These exercises require students to fill in the correct word in a sentence or a cloze story; match the meanings of sentences; categorize words according to themes in the story; match parts of sentences; unscramble sentences to form correct ones; and use context clues to fill in correct words from the main story. Encourage students to master the words in the exercises. They might explain the vocabulary in their own words and then use it to create new sentences about their own experiences. In categorizing exercises, have students brainstorm additional words for the given categories.

Some lessons contain sequencing activities that check general comprehension and help students analyze and think critically about a story line or theme. In many lessons, an exercise requires students to analyze and evaluate choices in food, student activities, family rules, or similar items related to the topic of the story. Other exercises focus on identifying what is appropriate to say in specified situations.

Each lesson contains a dialog based on the story. The dialog can be heard on the audio recording. The dialog models what might be said in an effective conversation about the subject. Have students listen before reading the dialog. Play the recording several times if necessary. Check comprehension and discuss content. Then play the recording again; stop after each line, and have students repeat what was said. This activity prepares students to act out the dialog themselves and provides useful pronunciation modeling and practice. Students can then practice with partners, creating role-plays featuring parents, teachers, and other school personnel. Encourage them to create new conversations on related topics, for example, by replacing key words or phrases in the dialog. For additional support, these new conversations can be written on the board for students to copy and practice.

Most lessons have a listening or reading activity. Listening activities are based on phone messages parents might receive from a child's school. Reading activities are based on letters or notices that might be sent home from school. These items are designed to increase understanding and let students practice appropriate responses to answering-machine messages, letters, forms, and other school information. Prompts for listening exercises are on the audio recordings. They are also printed at the end of the student book so that you can read them if a recording is not available, or you can have students prompt each other. The printed prompts also provide a way for students to check their responses. In level 2, follow-up questions give students an opportunity to verify their understanding by writing answers, discussing their answers, or writing notes to the child's teacher.

Other activities give students opportunities to fill out forms, create lists, correctly identify pictures, and answer questions about school-related documents, such as a medical brochure, a homework schedule, and a spelling test.

Many lessons include activities (*Problem Solving*) that focus attention on various difficult situations a parent may encounter (e.g., how to get a child up in the morning or how to help a shy child feel more comfortable in a new school). These are particularly effective when students work in small groups. Delegate responsibilities to a leader, recorder, and reporter in each group. In whole-class follow-up sessions, have students compare and discuss their suggestions as a way to expand their perspectives and find new solutions to particular dilemmas.

Exercises on the last page of many lessons (*Answer the Questions*) may be done individually if you prefer, but are most effective as prompts for class or group discussion. Encourage students to go beyond simple, short answers and explain or give details. Point out ways in which they can follow up on a partner's answer with questions of their own.

Discussion topics (*Discuss with a Partner*) can be used to stimulate whole-class or small-group discussion. Select topics that relate to themes students are working on, or allow students to select the topics that interest them most.

The topics can also stimulate written response. Write down what students say if they are not yet ready to write independently. Remember that students at this level may respond to a writing topic with only a few sentences or even just a few words or phrases.

Using *From Home to School 1* and *2 Workbooks*

The workbooks that accompany *From Home to School 1* and *2* are designed for the needs of English language learners but may also be useful to native speakers. The workbooks provide focused practice on specific language points from corresponding student book lessons. The purpose is to strengthen a student's abilities in listening, speaking, reading, and writing, with an emphasis on language for typical interactions between parents, children, and school personnel. For each lesson, workbook activities include grammar, vocabulary, focused listening exercises, spelling, and pronunciation practice.

Each lesson highlights selected grammar structures from the story. Exercises provide practice with giving short answers, asking tag questions, using verbs correctly, writing questions, using comparative adjectives, and the like.

Vocabulary-building activities include matching words with pictures, identifying words from the story, and matching sentences that mean the same.

Listening exercises, either word- or picture-based, are included in each lesson. In some exercises, students use oral cues to identify pictures and develop listening discrimination skills. Other listening exercises call for transcribing information such as times, prices, and dates; spelling words; and supplying words missing from sentences. Prompts for these exercises are on the audio recording and are also available at the end of the workbook. An answer key is provided as well. You should note that some workbook exercise items can have more than one correct answer. Only the most commonly used phrasing is given in the answer key.

In addition, the workbook offers pronunciation practice, with exercises focusing on particular vowel and consonant sounds, stressed syllables, and the pronunciation of plural forms. It also has activities in phonics, spelling, and punctuation.

All these exercises can provide effective practice for students working alone, in pairs, in small groups, or as a whole class.

Lesson Notes

The notes for each lesson have two sections, Preview and Exercises. Preview lists the main content messages and themes of the story. It also suggests warm-up activities, focusing on key concepts and vocabulary needed to understand the story. Preview activities let students draw on prior experience and share ideas or knowledge about issues in the story.

The Exercises section suggests ways to prepare for and carry out the exercises that follow the stories. The lesson notes may not refer to every activity, particularly those that are very easy to follow. Where appropriate, however, the notes suggest ways to expand activities or extend them to other contexts.

Literacy Lesson Notes

Lesson 1: Don't Miss the Bus

Preview

This story stresses the importance of being on time for school. It also addresses the theme of daily routines, focusing on morning activities such as getting up and getting ready for school. It includes references to transportation and almost missing the school bus.

Details in this story offer the opportunity to teach or review numbers in the context of time. Elicit from students what time they or their children get up in the morning. List various times on the board. Point to different examples and model the question "What time is it?" Listen for correct responses.

Explain the meaning of *tired* or additional feelings vocabulary that might pertain to the story. Ask, "Emily is tired in the morning. How does her father feel? How does your child feel in the morning? How do you feel?"

Brainstorm a list of objects commonly found in a child's bedroom. Make sure *alarm clock* is included in the list, and either bring one in or show a picture. Ask students if alarm clocks are used in their homes. Have students role-play a scene where one student wakes up another using the expression "Get up!"

List activities that people routinely do in the morning. Consider the amount of time that each task takes (e.g., eat breakfast: 10 minutes, get dressed: 5 minutes, etc.).

Show pictures of different means of transportation and elicit responses about how students or their children get to school.

Introduce or review other key vocabulary as needed (e.g., *bed, get up, breakfast, teeth, hair, run, late, wait, door, lucky*).

Exercises (pages 5–7)

Check yes or no about you. When responses are negative, have students provide answers, if possible, to information questions. Ask, "Where are you at 6:45? How do you feel in the morning? What meals do you eat? How do you get to school?"

Calling School This dialog can be used as a model for calling school about a child for a variety of reasons (e.g., lateness, absence, missing a particular activity, etc.). After modeling the dialog, pair students and encourage them to use their names or their children's names to create new dialogs. Listen for correct identification and spelling.

What do they say? Expand this activity by introducing other words or phrases to use in each scene (e.g., *"Stop!"* and *"Don't go!"* can be used as well as *"Wait!"*).

Lesson 2: My Head Itches

Preview

This story addresses the health theme, focusing on the identification and transmission of head lice. It also mentions how important it is to send home a child who has lice and keep the child home to avoid spreading lice to the rest of the class.

Students should know that a health issue such as lice can cause embarrassment. However, this is a common probem.

Details in this story offer the opportunity to teach or review vocabulary for body parts (particularly on the head), hair, personal clothing, and accessories such as hats and hairbrushes.

Model scratching your head, or refer to the first picture in the story showing a boy scratching his head in the classroom. Elicit or teach a response to the question "What's the matter?" (e.g., "My head itches. I have head lice. He has head lice.").

Examine head lice by using a photo or the drawing at the conclusion of the story. Make sure that students understand that nits are lice eggs. Have students predict places where a person with head lice might go (e.g., nurse's office, home, doctor's office, pharmacy, etc.) and, if possible, the steps necessary for treatment.

Demonstrate how head lice can be transmitted by showing a hairbrush, comb, hat, or scarf. And role-play the concept of *sharing* by pretending to offer one of the items to one of the students. Elicit names of other places one might find lice (e.g., on pillows, blankets, furniture, etc.).

Introduce or review other key vocabulary as needed (e.g., *class, itches, schoolwork, nurse, lice, nits, eggs, home, parents, share, hats, hairbrushes*).

Exercises (pages 9–11)

Check yes or no about you. Put students in small groups to brainstorm additional items that are good and bad to share. Have them list as many items as possible in each category. Check spelling and pronunciation.

Calling School This dialog may be used as a model for reporting any child's health issue to the school (e.g., cold, fever, chicken pox, flu, strep throat, etc.). Distinguish conditions that are particularly important to report because they are infectious or transmittable.

What shampoo do I buy? Consider bringing in a regular shampoo as well as one for the treatment of head lice. Compare information on the labels. Demonstrate items that might be included with the head lice product, like a fine-tooth comb, and explain their purpose (e.g., for removing eggs). Reading and understanding the directions for using the product may be a practical expansion of this lesson.

Lesson 3: A New Girl at School

Preview

This story addresses the themes of personal identification and feelings. Specific issues include facing the first day at a new school, dealing with language problems, and making friends.

Elicit names of countries represented by students in class and the names of languages spoken. On a map or globe, identify these countries, as well as the country mentioned in the story (Mexico).

Teach or review the correct response to the question "What is your name?" (e.g., "My name is _____."). Encourage students to practice both question and answer with a partner. Introduce additional information questions (e.g., "Where are you from? How old are you? What language do you speak?"), and model answers. When either

question or answer is unclear, encourage students to say, "I don't understand."

A line in this story, "Carmen sits next to Angela," offers the opportunity to teach or review prepositions. Use classroom seating to reinforce this concept (e.g., "Enrique sits next to Yukio," etc.).

Use the picture on the first page of the story to brainstorm other items commonly found in an elementary school classroom (e.g., calendar, desk, flag, etc.).

Introduce or review other key vocabulary as needed (e.g., *years, speaks, first, shy, everyone, children, sits, next to, nice, new, friend*).

Exercises (pages 13–15)

Check yes or no about you. Encourage students from other countries to make negative sentences followed by corrected positive sentences (e.g., "I am not from Mexico. I am from Japan. I don't speak Spanish. I speak Japanese.").

Meeting the Teacher This dialog may be used as a model for introducing one person to another in other situations. Arrange students in groups of three for additional dialog practice. Substitute *son* for *daughter* when appropriate. Change roles so everyone has a chance to make an introduction. Note that the expression "Don't worry" may be used to offer comfort or assurance in other instances as well.

Complete the sentences. Question 2 addresses making a child feel more comfortable in school. If possible, have students suggest other ways a parent can ease a child's transition into a new school.

Lesson 4: Breakfast at School

Preview

This story stresses the importance of eating breakfast before school. Specific issues include parental concern, feeling ready to study before or after eating, and the names of some breakfast foods.

Elicit names of some common breakfast foods or particular foods that students or their children eat in the morning.

Teach or review the vocabulary for mealtime (e.g., *breakfast, lunch, dinner*). Ask how many meals students eat every day and what time they eat. Elicit responses as to which meals they eat at home or away (e.g., "I eat breakfast at home. I eat lunch at school.").

Brainstorm a list of things that a parent wants a child to do before leaving for school (e.g., eat, take a shower, brush teeth, put on a jacket, pack homework, etc.).

Discuss how people may feel when they do not eat (e.g., hungry, tired, irritable, weak, etc.) and how they may feel after eating (e.g., full, better, happy, etc.).

Find out if a school breakfast or lunch program is available at your school site. Obtain a menu from the school cafeteria or from another school that offers a meal program. (Menus are often available on school web sites.)

Introduce or review other key vocabulary as needed (e.g., *breakfast, leaving, kitchen, box, cereal, want, time, study, ready, hungry, pancakes, orange juice, feels, better*).

Exercises (pages 17–19)

Check yes or no about you. Consider expanding the expression of likes and dislikes (e.g., "I like pancakes. I don't like scrambled eggs."). If possible, practice in the third person (e.g., "My son likes cereal. He doesn't like yogurt.").

Reading the School Breakfast Menu Issue copies of a school menu to students for comprehension practice. Ask, "When are they having scrambled eggs? What are they having on Wednesday?" Have students say whether or not they would want to eat at school based on the menu.

Lesson 5: Read More at Home

Preview

This story emphasizes the importance of reading for success in school. It also demonstrates that a parent-teacher conference is an occasion for learning how well a child is doing in school. Themes include concern for a child whose reading skills are behind the rest of the class and using a convenient resource (e.g., school or community library) for additional reading materials.

A time reference in this story offers the opportunity to teach or review numbers. Elicit from students possible times for meeting with their child's teacher. Explain *before* and *after* school, making distinctions between A.M. and P.M.

List some adjectives that describe positive classroom behavior (e.g., *nice, good, polite, pleasant, kind, considerate*, etc.). Also discuss the meaning of *behind* as it pertains to a child's performance in a particular area.

Elicit names of school subjects (e.g., reading, math, social studies, science, etc.). Explain the meanings of these subjects if necessary. Have students express opinions about whether or not a particular subject is difficult for them.

Introduce or review other key vocabulary as needed (e.g., *mother, father, talking, teacher, boy, problem, difficult, behind, more, home, library, important, reader*).

Exercises (pages 21–23)

Check yes or no about you. After completing item 2, discuss how much time the students or the students' children spend reading at home each day. Ask where reading takes place (e.g., living room, bedroom, kitchen, etc.). Ask if there is time to read more at home. After item 4, discuss borrowing books from a library. Ask if students have library cards or have gone to a library. List other things that can be borrowed. Elicit responses about items that might be good or bad to borrow.

Talking to the Teacher This dialog may be used as a model for inquiring about school in general or areas of particular concern (e.g., "How is my child doing in math? How is my child doing in physical education?").

Complete the sentences. After completing item 2, brainstorm other places in your community for borrowing or buying reading material.

Lesson 6: A Classroom Volunteer

Preview

This story makes the point that parents are encouraged or expected to volunteer in their child's classroom. It refers to a set schedule and describes duties that a parent volunteer may perform: assisting with small groups, explaining lessons to students who ask for help, handing out papers, and other activities that support the teacher.

Teach or review the days of the week and time vocabulary. Use a calendar to point out every Tuesday in a month to indicate when the volunteer in the story is at school. Elicit information from any parent volunteers about days and times they help at school.

Cluster some students together and indicate that they are a group. Demonstrate that a group can be small or large. Also, hand out papers to explain the reference in the story. Ask students what other objects are handed out in class (e.g., pencils, books, notices, etc.).

Raise your hand, and elicit responses as to the meaning of the signal (e.g., "I need help. I don't understand. I have a question."). Ask students to share other gestures or expressions that indicate a need for assistance.

Introduce or review other key vocabulary as needed (e.g., *volunteer, daughter, class, every, group, flash card, addition, understand, raises, helps, handing out, papers, proud*).

Exercises (pages 25–27)

Check yes or no about you. Discuss item 4, and explain that feelings are not always the same. Ask, "Mrs. Yong's daughter feels proud. How does your child feel when you come to school?" Elicit some possible feelings vocabulary for the situation (e.g., *happy, embarrassed, excited, worried,* etc.).

Helping a Student Teach or review some basic arithmetic terms, such as *addition, subtraction, plus,* and *minus.* Use flash cards, if possible, to demonstrate the spoken language in an addition problem (e.g., "Five plus two equals seven."). Have students work with a partner and practice reading several addition problems.

Lesson 7: The Report Card

Preview

This story addresses the issue of receiving a report card in the mail and having difficulty understanding it. Specific problems include interpreting letter and number grades and teacher's comments. Other elements are the feeling of confusion and the need to seek help.

Obtain a report card and envelope from your school site if possible. Open the envelope and identify the report card. Ask students how many times in a school year report cards for their children are produced. Then ask if the report cards are mailed, received at a conference, or hand-delivered by the child.

Consider filling out a sample report card following the guidelines of your school site. Discuss what letter or number grades mean. Clarify the different subjects or behaviors for which students receive grades or comments.

Teacher's comments may be particularly hard to understand. Ask students if translators or other services are provided at their children's schools for parents who cannot speak or read English well.

Introduce or review other key vocabulary as needed (e.g., *standing, mailbox, mail, letter, envelope, report card, letters, numbers, comments, words, understand, inside, apartment, confused, help*). Explain that *letter,* in this story, can mean either *letter in the mail* or *letter of the alphabet.*

Exercises (pages 29–31)

Check yes or no about you. Discuss item 3, eliciting other reasons for calling your child's school (e.g., explaining absence or tardiness, etc.). Ask students if a person in the school office speaks their native language. Have students name other people (e.g., husband, wife, children, other relatives, friends, neighbors, etc.) who help them get information, ask questions, or communicate concerns regarding their school-age children. For item 4, brainstorm a list of other places where students may need translators (e.g., clinic, hospital, government office, etc.).

Calling the School Office This can also be a model for requesting help when students do not understand other school-related items that they receive in the mail or from their children (e.g., health notices, field trip announcements, dress code revisions, permission slips, etc.). Have students practice asking and answering the last question in the dialog, substituting their native language for Russian if necessary (e.g., "Do you need a translator? Yes, I need a Spanish translator.").

Lesson 8: Sign Up for Soccer

Preview

This story addresses a child's requests to participate in after-school activities, play soccer, and engage in activities with peers, as well as parental uncertainty and fact-finding.

Elicit information regarding organized youth sports in the community (e.g., soccer, basketball, baseball, etc.). Consider charting a few examples listing name of the sport, day, time, place, and cost.

Sport	Day	Time	Place	Cost
Soccer	Tuesday	4:00–6:00	Helix Field	$90

Teach or review appropriate information questions (e.g., "What sport is it? What day is it? What time is it? Where is it? How much is it?"). Have students practice questions and answers with partners.

Ask students to list places their children are usually picked up (e.g., school, sports field, movie theater, a friend's house, etc.). Ask students if other people sometimes pick up their children. Elicit relationships of the people who sometimes pick up their children (e.g., grandparent, friend, neighbor, etc.).

A clothing reference in this story offers the opportunity to teach or review names of clothing, particularly parts of uniforms or other specialized clothing for sports (e.g., *jersey, shorts, soccer cleats, knee pads, socks*, etc.).

Ask students if they sometimes call the parents of their children's friends. Elicit information on how to obtain phone numbers (e.g., looking up numbers in a school handbook or telephone directory, asking people for their numbers, etc.).

Introduce or review other key vocabulary as needed (e.g., *sitting, car, picking up, after, excited,*

play, soccer, friends, neighborhood, wear, uniforms, fun, day, time, place, money, costs, parents).

Exercises (pages 33–35)

Check yes or no about you. For items 1 and 2, elicit information regarding other sports students enjoy either playing or watching. Ask which sports are popular in their native countries. Ask if children can play these sports.

Calling Another Parent The first line of this dialog may be used as a model for contacting another parent for any reason. Encourage students to practice saying the line, substituting their own first and last names, child's name, and relationship to the child (e.g., "Hello, Mr. Ruiz. This is Elena Cortez, Pedro's grandmother.").

Who wants to play soccer? Gather some announcements for sports or other after-school activities. Circulate flyers in the classroom, or project them on an overhead. Have students identify the sport or activity, as well as the day, time, location, and cost of participation.

Lesson 9: Fighting at School

Preview

This story addresses the serious issue of fighting at school. Details include a parent recognizing that her child has been in a conflict, finding out who was responsible, then reporting the problem to the school principal and understanding that there will be consequences.

Teach or review other expressions to use in addition to "What's the matter?" (e.g., "What's wrong? What happened? Why are you crying?").

This story refers to expressing emotion (e.g., crying) and giving reassurance in the form of a hug. Ask students about things that upset their children or make them cry (e.g., getting hurt, feeling disappointment, arguing, etc.) and other things a parent can do to offer comfort.

Explain fighting terms used in the story and others that describe physical confrontations (*hit, kick, push, punch, slap, elbow*, etc.). Teach or review ways to respond to this type of incident (e.g., Don't hit back. Tell the teacher.).

Discuss the possibility of contacting other school authorities (e.g., teacher, vice-principal, counselor, etc.) regarding problems at school. Remind students to report extremely serious problems to the police.

Consider other actions that can get a child in trouble at school (e.g., stealing, vandalizing, cheating, harassing, etc.).

Introduce or review other key vocabulary as needed (e.g., *face, dirty, torn, crying, mean, hit, kick, fight, afraid, hug, principal, son, trouble, bad*).

Exercises (pages 37–39)

Check yes or no about you. This activity offers an opportunity to review other words for feelings. This is a good time to address the feelings of both parent and child in the context of school (e.g., "I feel confused at school. My daughter feels happy at school.").

Calling the Principal Use the dialog as a model. Have students role-play to practice using the terms *mother, father, son, daughter, his,* and *her* correctly. Have male and female students in the class use the terms *mother* and *father* appropriately. Remind students to use *his* or *her* when referring to their sons or daughters.

Lesson 10:
He Can't Do Multiplication

Preview

This story stresses the idea that parents can play an active role in supporting their children academically. Issues include recognizing that a child is struggling in a particular area and taking steps to provide assistance. The message is that working together at home can be an effective way to strengthen skills in the classroom.

Teach or review the mathematical term *multiplication*. Then explain how the word *times* is used in math, and do some sample exercises modeling multiplication questions (e.g., "What is two times three?").

Demonstrate two ways of solving a multiplication problem. First, simply elicit memorized responses from students (e.g., "Two times three is six."). Next show confusion (e.g., "I don't know."),

and attempt to solve the problem by counting on your fingers. Have students identify each method as either *fast* or *slow*.

Show a packet of multiplication flash cards. Say that flash cards can help children memorize the problems so they can give answers the *fast* way. Brainstorm locations where these or other materials for school are available (e.g., teacher supply store, office supply store, large discount department store, etc.).

Ask who provides help at home when a child has a problem at school (e.g., parents, siblings, relatives, other school friends, etc.). Discuss subjects that may be difficult and others that are easy. Model comparisons for students to practice (e.g., "Math is difficult, but reading is easy.").

A reference to the *table* in this story may lead to a discussion about other places in the home where children work (e.g., desk, sofa, floor, bed, etc.).

Introduce or review other key vocabulary as needed (e.g., *multiplication, homework, count, fingers, slow, help, idea, school supply store, flash cards, pick up, practice, table, evening, quickly, fun, easy*).

Exercises (pages 41–43)

Check yes or no about you. After completing item 4, encourage students to list specific subjects in which they can provide homework assistance (e.g., "I can help my child with reading. I can help my child with math.").

Looking for Flash Cards In the last line, *next to* offers the opportunity to teach or review prepositions, particularly those that pinpoint the location of something on a store shelf (e.g., *above, below, next to, between, behind, on the left, on the right,* etc.). Have students practice variations of the dialog by directing someone to flash cards in a new location.

Lesson 11: She Talks Too Much

Preview

This story addresses behavior problems at school and a teacher's efforts to discipline a misbehaving student. Other issues include talking during class and disrupting other students, annoying the teacher, changing seats, and carrying a note home from the teacher.

Details in this story offer the opportunity to teach or review emotion words, particularly ones relating to being angry and upset (e.g., *mad, annoyed, irritated, furious,* etc.).

Consider doing a role-play activity to act out the story. Have two students sitting next to each other talk. Direct one of the students to "Move to another seat" to make the concept clear. Direct the other student to continue talking to another nearby student. Then hand the talking student a note and say, "Give this to your mother and father." Ask students to predict how the parents of this student will feel. Brainstorm as many emotion words as possible.

Clarify *talk* and *tell* as used in the story. Explain that *talk* means to speak in general (e.g., "Hello. How are you?), and *tell,* in this case, means to give an order (e.g., "Stop talking.").

Introduce or review other key vocabulary as needed (e.g., *talking, recess, teacher, tells, stop, move, seat, working, quietly, angry, writes note, parents, upset*).

Exercises (pages 45–47)

Check yes or no about you. After completing item 4, elicit other things from a child's school that can upset parents (e.g., a bad report card, a phone call from the principal, etc.).

A Call from the Teacher Use this to model calls to parents about other behavior problems that might occur in school (e.g., She arrives late. She doesn't listen. She uses bad language.). Brainstorm disciplinary actions parents might take after a phone call like this (e.g., suspend TV or telephone privileges, make the child write a letter of apology to the teacher, etc.).

Lesson 12: It's Bedtime

Preview

This story stresses the message that children need a sufficient amount of sleep in order to function well at school. Issues include parents enforcing a school-night bedtime rule. A reference to a sleepy student shows the disadvantage of not getting enough rest.

Teach or review the term *bedtime rule,* and ask students if their children have a regular bedtime on school nights. Elicit responses about various bedtimes (e.g., "My child goes to bed at 8:30 on school nights.").

Demonstrate looking at the clock and pointing to the time. Ask students if they do this when it is time for their children to go to bed. Discuss how much time children need to get ready for bed, and list what they do (e.g., put on pajamas, brush teeth, etc.).

Ask students how many clocks they have at home and where the clocks are located (e.g., on the kitchen wall, on a table in the bedroom, etc.). Ask what activities their children are doing before getting ready for bed (e.g., doing homework, reading, watching TV, listening to music, playing games, etc.).

Brainstorm some problems a sleepy child may have at school (e.g., "He can't learn. He forgets things.").

Introduce or review other key vocabulary as needed (e.g., *game, sister, get ready, bed, school night, rule, tired, late, upstairs, comfortable*).

Exercises (pages 49–51)

Check yes or no about you. Have students discuss their bedtime routines. List various things students do to get ready for bed and how much time each activity takes (e.g., take a shower: 10 minutes, brush and floss teeth: 5 minutes, etc.).

Advice from the Teacher Encourage students to practice this dialog in pairs, inserting their own bedtimes.

Complete the sentences. As a follow-up activity to item 2, elicit responses from students about other family rules or rules for their children (e.g., when they can see friends, what foods they should not eat, when homework must be done, how much time they can spend on the telephone, etc.).

Lesson 13: Expensive Shoes

Preview

This story highlights a difference of opinion between a parent and child who are shopping for shoes. While the parent considers budget realities, the child is more concerned with peer reactions. Issues include making comparisons, spending money, and expressing feelings.

Teach or review adjective opposites especially as they pertain to prices or fashion (e.g., *cheap* or *expensive, high* or *low, pretty* or *ugly, popular* or *unpopular,* etc.).

Discuss buying shoes and clothing on sale. Ask students how they find out about sales (e.g., newspapers, TV, radio, mail, signs in store windows, etc.). Elicit responses about places in the community that have good prices on shoes and clothing for children.

Teach or review numbers between one and one hundred. Practice reading random dollar amounts. Elicit opinions about how much money is *too much* to spend on shoes.

Discuss brand names of shoes or clothing that are popular among schoolchildren or adults. Have students estimate prices of some of these items or, if they are comfortable sharing the information, tell what they have paid. Ask students if they usually select brand-name items or lower-cost alternatives (e.g., shoes, jeans, purses, accessories, etc.). Elicit opinions about whether or not discounted or off-brand items are the same or *almost* the same.

Review emotion words relevant to this story (e.g., *sad, angry, disappointed, upset, frustrated*).

Introduce or review other key vocabulary as needed (e.g., *shopping, shoe store, cheap, expensive, almost, same, nobody, too much, sad, angry*).

Exercises (pages 53–55)

Check yes or no about you. After completing item four, make a list of items in a child's standard school outfit. Elicit approximate dollar amounts for each item. Have students express opinions about the various prices (e.g., "I think $25 is too much for pants." or "I think $25 is OK for pants.").

At the Shoe Store The first two lines of this dialog may be used as a model to help students inquire about the price of any item. Have students replace the word *shoes* with names for other pieces of clothing. Point out the necessary grammatical changes when the word is singular (e.g., "How much is this shirt? It is only $12 on sale.").

Lesson 14: Playground Safety

Preview

This story underlines the messages that running on the playground can be dangerous and that there are consequences to violating safety rules. Themes include weather, weather-appropriate clothing, parts of the body, and the issue of coming to the assistance of an injured child.

References in this story (cold, jacket, knee) provide the opportunity to teach or review weather vocabulary, cold-weather clothing words, and words for body parts.

Show the picture at the beginning of the lesson to illustrate *recess.* Ask how much time children usually have for recess at school. Label some of the activities the children in the picture are engaged in (e.g., climbing, running, jumping, sliding, etc.). Discuss whether students' children play inside or outside when the weather is bad.

Indicate the soft (sand, grass, field) or hard (playground, blacktop) surfaces in both pictures illustrating the story. Discuss why running on the blacktop surface can be dangerous. Consider various recess activities and whether a soft or hard surface would be best for each. Ask parents to describe what playgrounds at their children's schools are like. Ask students if there are rules about activities children cannot do on playgrounds.

Ask students whether or not there is a nurse's office at their child's school. Teach or review some vocabulary for minor injuries that may be treated in a nurse's office (*scrapes, cuts, bloody noses,* etc.).

Brainstorm additional phrases to use when coming to the assistance of a child who is hurt or crying (e.g., "Are you OK? Are you all right? What happened? Where does it hurt?").

Introduce or review other key vocabulary as needed (e.g., *recess, playing, outside, cold, jacket, put on, run, fast, fall down, knee, crying, playground, nurse's office, dangerous*).

Exercises (pages 57–59)

Check yes or no about you. After item 2, have students work in pairs to describe what they are wearing and what their partners are wearing (e.g., "I am wearing a shirt and pants. She is wearing a sweater and skirt."). Add colors if possible.

Help from a Teacher on the Playground This dialog may be used as a model for specifying injuries to other parts of the body. Brainstorm words for body parts that children commonly injure (e.g., *elbow, hand, head, face, leg, arm,* etc.) to expand practice. Have students practice the dialog in pairs, substituting other body parts for the knee.

Lesson 15: Absent from School

Preview

This story stresses parental responsibility when a child is absent from school. Issues include recognizing symptoms to determine when a child is sick and unable to go to school and taking the necessary steps of calling the school, identifying the child, and reporting the reason for the absence.

Teach or review some common childhood illnesses that may prevent a child from attending school (e.g., fever, cough, cold, flu, sore throat, earache, stomachache, etc.).

Discuss identifying a fever either by touch or by using a thermometer. Interpret the meanings of the numbers on a Fahrenheit thermometer (e.g., Normal is 98.6 degrees.), and discuss whether or not it is good to send a child to school with particular readings above that. Ask students if their children's schools have rules about not sending children to school with fevers.

Discuss ways to treat children who are sick with a cold or the flu. Brainstorm a list of appropriate foods or liquids. Ask students what other things they do to take care of a sick child and how they can tell whether or not a child needs to see a doctor.

Discuss the number of days a child may be absent with a fever. Ask students how often their children are absent from school and why.

Introduce or review other key vocabulary as needed (e.g., *sick, thermometer, mouth, temperature, fever, stay home, attendance clerk, last name, grade, bed, rest*).

Exercises (pages 61–63)

Check yes or no about you. Discuss who calls the child's school, if not the student (e.g., husband, wife, daughter, son, etc.). If the answer to item 4 is no, discuss who stays home or where the child goes (e.g., "My son goes to my mother-in-law's house when he is sick.").

Too Sick to Go to School This dialog can be used as a model for reporting any illness. Have students practice reporting a child's absence from school. Encourage students to substitute their own child's name, identify the child as their *son* or *daughter,* and substitute names of various illnesses. Have students practice stating the child's name, correctly spelling out the last name, and identifying the child's grade.

Level 1 Lesson Notes

Lesson 1: Don't Miss the Bus

Preview

This story addresses themes of daily routine, getting up in the morning, school transportation, and almost missing the school bus.

Discuss what time students' children generally wake up. Ask if the children use an alarm clock, rely on parents, or get up independently.

Ask students to describe their children's daily routines, focusing particularly on what the children do in the morning before leaving for school. Discuss the amount of time children need to get ready. Provide vocabulary as needed.

Discuss how students' children get to school. If they take the bus, ask how far the bus stop is from home. Find out if the bus driver sometimes waits for children and what happens when a child misses the bus.

For ESL learners, introduce or review other key vocabulary as needed (e.g., *tired, sleep, miss, school bus, minutes, combs, backpack, corner, move, lucky*).

Exercises (pages 6–9)

Complete the Story After students complete the cloze story, ask questions to check comprehension. Encourage students to write or tell a story about someone getting up in the morning. Students may use the story in this activity as a model.

Late Again After students listen to the dialog, ask questions to check comprehension. Role-plays can create typical exchanges between a parent and a child getting ready for school in the morning.

A Message from the Principal After students listen to the message and complete the exercise, ask questions to check comprehension. Extend the activity by asking questions (e.g., "Why is this a serious problem? How would you react if you were Marc's parent? Have you ever had this problem? How did you solve it?"). Students can role-play a telephone conversation on various topics between a parent and a school principal.

Discuss with a Partner In Topic 3, elicit discussion about whether or not it is a parent's responsibility to get a child up and ready for school on time. If possible, have students take positions on the topic and debate. Encourage them to look at the question from the perspective of different people (e.g., a parent, a teacher, a child, etc.).

Lesson 2: An Eye Exam

Preview

This story addresses themes of health, routine examinations at school, and parent notification.

Discuss symptoms that could indicate a vision problem. Encourage students to talk about their own experience with having their eyes tested. Ask questions to elicit details of students' experience (e.g., "Where did the test occur? How was the test performed? What did the test show?").

Examine the role of a nurse or health aide at school. Ask students to share information they have received about health screenings or related announcements at school. Elicit and practice appropriate responses to these notices.

Review ordinal numbers if necessary. For ESL learners, introduce or review other key vocabulary as needed (e.g., *nurse, exams, turn, chart, line, board, copy, wrong, headache, worry*). Also, review *below, left,* and *right* as they are used in the story.

Exercises (pages 12–15)

Complete the Sentences Have students create new sentences, using the exercise sentences as models (e.g., "Please cover your right eye and read. Please cover your left eye. Please open your right eye.").

Matching After students match each sentence, discuss when or where a person might use these expressions.

Parents Talking After students listen to the dialog, ask questions to check comprehension (e.g., "Who is the letter from? What does it say? Does their daughter need glasses? What do the parents need to do?"). Extend this activity by having students suggest how to find a vision care professional.

Family Eye Care Check general understanding of the information in this advertisement. After students complete and check the exercise, have them compare three or four advertisements from the local yellow pages. Ask students which place they would consider going to for an eye exam and why.

Lesson 3: A New Girl at School

Preview

This story addresses themes of the first day at a new school, introductions, language problems, and making friends.

Elicit names of countries represented by the students in class, either native countries or ancestral ones, and the names of languages spoken. On a map, identify these countries, as well as the country mentioned in the story.

Encourage students to discuss their memories of being new students or experiences their children may have had, particularly if they involved instruction in a new language. Discuss ways to prepare children for different kinds of transitions. Review words for emotions, especially those that children sometimes feel at school.

Talk about ways that children make friends with each other. Encourage students to share a memory of a playmate from elementary school.

For ESL learners, introduce or review other key vocabulary as needed (e.g., *enters, welcome, shy, understand, empty, worry, came, easy, smiles, better*).

Exercises (pages 18–21)

Complete the Story After students complete the cloze story, ask questions to check comprehension. Encourage students to recall instances when either they or their children misunderstood some direction given at school.

Check the Feelings After completing the activity have students say or circle the words that describe positive feelings. Encourage students to recount a time when they felt one of the emotions listed.

Meeting the Teacher After students listen to the dialog, ask questions to check comprehension.

Encourage students to role-play another exchange between a teacher and the parent of a new student.

Personal Information Form Expand this activity by using a student information form from a local school. Assist students in writing more challenging personal information.

Make a List After listing items, encourage students to explain their reasons why an item is or is not good to bring to school.

Discuss with a Partner In Topic 2, elicit from students their experiences with language learning, as children or as adults. Discuss the challenges of language learning at different ages. Ask, "What are the advantages or disadvantages of learning a language (or any new skill) as an adult? What kinds of things are easier for children to adjust to?"

Lesson 4: Breakfast at School

Preview

This story addresses themes of getting ready for school, breakfast food, transportation, time management, and school breakfast programs.

Review or teach names of the food items referred to in the story and other common breakfast foods. Elicit or teach names of containers or quantities that are associated with the way these foods are usually bought or served.

Discuss the reasons for eating regular meals and the importance of breakfast in particular.

Have students share information about what meals and what kinds of foods are available at their children's schools. Provide or have students bring in menus (often available from school web sites) for breakfast and/or lunch from various schools.

For ESL learners, introduce or review other key vocabulary as needed (e.g., *ready, catch, bowl, piece, program, healthy, hungry, cafeteria, bell, container*).

Exercises (pages 24–27)

Underline the Word from the Story Have students write new sentences using the words in parentheses. Encourage them to write or tell a story beginning with sentence 1: "It's early in the morning. . . ."

What's for Breakfast? Expand this activity by using a school menu from a local school. Have students substitute actual breakfast or lunch information from that menu in creating new dialogs. Encourage students to express whether they like or dislike various items on the school menu.

This Week's Breakfast Menu Discuss the nutritional value in each selection. Ask students which selection their child would or would not eat.

Lesson 5: Read More at Home

Preview

This story addresses themes of parent-teacher conferences, student evaluation, the importance of reading, and study habits at home.

Elicit information regarding parent-teacher conferences at various schools. Ask what time of year and what time of day conferences generally take place. Discuss whether one or both parents should attend conferences and why. Ask if the services of a translator are available. List reasons why some parents cannot or do not attend conferences.

Elicit and discuss common concerns parents have about their children in school. Also discuss issues that a teacher may raise about a child's performance or behavior.

Ask students what their children like to do in their free time. Discuss methods of redirecting children to practice skills that improve schoolwork.

Bring in a flyer or other information about the public library in your community. Discuss the library's location and hours. Review names for types of books that can be found there.

For ESL learners, introduce or review key vocabulary as needed (e.g., *conference, smile, proud, behind, worried, explains, library, check out*).

Exercises (pages 30–33)

What Is the Category? Identify the duties of various school personnel. Have students discuss instances when a person feels the emotions listed. Have students mention school subjects that they or their children find challenging.

Check the Books Gather and bring in examples of books from different categories. Have students

help identify the type of book (children's, mystery, biography, science, etc.) and where it might be found in the library.

Checking Out Books Encourage students to create new dialogs based on the rules their public library has about obtaining a library card, whether or not books can be borrowed immediately, and when books need to be returned.

Discuss with a Partner In Topic 3, encourage students to bring in favorite children's books to share with the class. Have students discuss the theme and characters of the book they brought with a partner. If possible, have a student read a passage aloud. Encourage other students to ask the reader questions.

Lesson 6: A Classroom Volunteer

Preview

This story addresses themes of volunteering in a classroom, duties of a parent volunteer, practicing addition, and the benefits of being a classroom volunteer.

Discuss the kinds of responsibilities that a volunteer might have at different grade levels. Ask students who have acted as volunteers to share their experiences. Ask what their duties were, if they worked directly with children, and if they enjoyed what they did. Have volunteers explain how their work was beneficial.

Review some basic arithmetic terms, such as *addition* and *subtraction*. Use flash cards if possible to demonstrate the numerical representation of spoken language in an addition problem (e.g., "Five plus two equals seven.") Have students practice several examples.

Review days of the week and time vocabulary if necessary. Calculate intervals of time for additional practice.

For ESL learners, introduce or review key vocabulary as needed (e.g., *grade, volunteer, raises, corrects, groups, learn, addition, flash cards, proud, spend time*).

Exercises (pages 36–39)

Unscramble the Sentences After students unscramble the sentences, demonstrate how the words in sentence 1 can also form a question. Point out the needed changes in capitalization and punctuation.

Helping in Class Encourage students to create new dialogs based on activities they might do in their children's classes. Review various tasks, such as handing out papers, making copies, hanging up artwork on a bulletin board, cutting out letters or numbers, and cleaning up.

Who Needs Help? Have students describe exactly what each child is doing. Ask how they know that a child needs or does not need help.

Make a List Ask students to explain why they like or dislike a certain classroom activity. Discuss their experiences with specific jobs and how they felt at the time. For example: "I didn't like going to the office and making copies for the teacher. It was a boring job. I prefer to work with the children in the classroom when I volunteer."

Discuss with a Partner In Topic 2, encourage students to contact local schools and ask about volunteer opportunities both in class and in other settings. Have them share and discuss ideas they get from the schools.

Lesson 7: Tests Next Week

Preview

This story addresses themes of school testing, parent notification, and preparation for testing.

Have students share information about what kinds of notices their children bring home from school. If possible, collect or have students bring in various notices to use as examples.

Discuss standardized tests that are routinely given at school. Elicit information about the names of these tests, the grades in which they are given, the time of year tests are usually taken, the number of days children are tested, the subjects that are covered, reports of test results, etc. Students can create a chart presenting this information as a guide for further discussion and as a reference to what their children will face.

Encourage students to share their views on the effectiveness of standardized tests and whether or not these tests always show what children know.

Discuss measures that parents can take to prepare their children for testing. Bring up issues of food, particularly breakfast, and amounts of sleep that children should have. Talk about consequences of being hungry or tired during testing.

Introduce or review vocabulary for school subjects (*reading, math, language arts, science,* etc.) if necessary.

Exercises (pages 42–45)

Complete the Sentences Have students use the exercise sentences as models to make new sentences for extra vocabulary practice (e.g., "The teacher suggests that you eat a good breakfast. The teacher suggests that you arrive at school on time.").

Matching It may be necessary to review some grammar and basic sentence structure to help students complete the exercise. Have them follow up by creating new sentences using each beginning phrase.

Check the Papers Have students share examples of specific documents and notices within these categories (e.g., "My daughter brought home a permission slip for a class field trip to the zoo."). Elicit reactions to different notices (e.g., "I was concerned when I got the notice about chicken pox going around the second grade class.").

Rest before the Test Create new dialogs between a parent and an uncooperative child. Ask, "What do parents do with a child who is unwilling to go to bed?" Discuss how a parent can explain the importance of testing.

Discuss with a Partner In Topic 2, encourage students to share a time when they were surprised by a child's tests results. Ask, "Did you think the test was fair? What did you do?"

Lesson 8: Sign Up for Soccer

Preview

This story addresses themes of a child's request to participate in after-school activities, playing soccer, engaging in activities with peers, parental uncertainty, and fact-finding.

Elicit information regarding youth sports and opportunities to participate at local recreation centers or through community organizations. Ask students about their children's participation in a sport or other activity: "What do they play or do? Where do these activities take place? How often does the child participate? What is the cost? How are parents involved?"

Have students share concerns they have had about involvement in extracurricular activities. Discuss possible concerns about money, time, transportation, risk of injury, supervision, etc.

Ask students whether or not they know the parents of their children's friends. Ask if there have been occasions when it was necessary to call them, and if so, why. Elicit reasons to make contact either in person or on the telephone. Ask students who have had such contacts to describe the conversations.

Brainstorm ways to give hesitant or ambiguous answers to questions (e.g., "We'll see." or "Possibly."). Discuss why these answers are sometimes easier than more definite yes or no responses.

For ESL learners, introduce or review other key vocabulary as needed (e.g., *sign up, youth center, soccer, football, uniforms, information, practice, games*).

Exercises (pages 48–51)

Complete the Story After students complete the story, have them compare common youth sports such as soccer and basketball. Ask, "How is each game played? Which game is more enjoyable to play or watch?"

Check the Sports Discuss the activities listed, and explain any that are unclear. Bring in pictures of the sports if possible. Have students express their opinions on various activities. Discuss which ones are the most expensive to participate in and why, which provides the most exercise, and which is the most dangerous, the most fun, or the most popular.

Calling a Parent for Information Have students create dialogs or role-plays about other reasons to contact another parent outside of school, such as a class trip or an upcoming meeting at the school.

Discuss with a Partner In Topic 2, discuss the benefits of allowing children to do what their friends are doing. Elicit instances when students did not allow their child to participate in something and why.

Lesson 9: Fighting at School

Preview

This story addresses themes of bullying or harassment, fighting at school, emotions, parental concern, and reporting a problem to the school principal.

Ask students how they know when something is bothering their children. Discuss signs such as a loss of appetite or being more emotional than usual.

Bring in a sample school handbook, and review the section about school rules. Discuss policies about harassment or violence at school. Discuss other school rules, and rank them in order of seriousness. This discussion may be started as a preview activity, then continued and expanded after reading the story and completing at least some of the lesson activities.

Discuss events that involved conflict between students' children and other children. Encourage students to recall what happened and how the conflicts were resolved.

Review titles of school personnel if necessary. Ask which person a parent should contact to report a case of harassment or a similar problem. Discuss appropriate ways of reporting problems, such as face-to-face meetings, telephone calls, or letters.

For ESL learners, introduce or review other key vocabulary as needed (e.g., *dirty, torn, cry, afraid, surprised, upset, fight, hit, kick, hug, trouble, rules*).

Exercises (pages 54–57)

Matching After students match the sentences, encourage them to create new pairs of sentences with similar meanings that might be useful when dealing with problem situations (e.g., "What's the problem?" and "What's bothering you?").

Reporting a Problem Create new dialogs based on other infractions of school rules. Review a school handbook for ideas or draw on experiences of students and their children.

School Rules Expand this activity by having students write rules that their children need to follow at home.

Discuss with a Partner In Topic 3, encourage students to discuss problems their children have had with other children at school.

Lesson 10: Too Tired for Homework

Preview

This story addresses themes of time management, homework, playing, and parental control.

Have students discuss various ways in which their children avoid doing homework. Encourage students to share ways that they procrastinate when they do not want to do something.

Ask students how much homework their children have and how it is managed at home. Ask, "Is there a certain time of day that homework needs to be done? When is it? How do you make sure that homework is being done? What happens if it isn't completed?"

Discuss the issue of allowing children some time after school to rest or play before doing homework. Ask how much free time is suitable before having children start on their homework.

For ESL learners, introduce or review other key vocabulary as needed (e.g., *homework, later, mirror, faces, angry, wasting, tired, toys*).

Exercises (pages 60–63)

Complete the Sentences Have students use the exercise sentences as models to make new sentences for extra vocabulary practice. Encourage students to write about their own experience.

Check the Activities Encourage students to give specific examples of the TV programs, toys, reading material, sports, and music their children enjoy. Ask why the children enjoy these or other activities listed.

Homework Comes First Have students create new dialogs in which parents respond to children who want to do something besides homework. Discuss what comes first in their families: homework or other family obligations.

This Week's Homework Have parents bring in a child's homework schedule and share it with the class. Discuss whether the amount of homework seems reasonable.

Discuss with a Partner In Topic 1, discuss methods of solving homework problems when you are unable to assist your child. Ask students if they ever had this experience and what they did. If appropriate, bring in information about local or online homework assistance services.

Lesson 11: Listen and Follow Directions

Preview

This story addresses themes of paying attention in class, following directions, test-taking, daydreaming, and receiving a warning from the teacher.

Discuss the subject of spelling tests and how often they are given. Ask how many words are typically on a test. Discuss ways of helping a child prepare for a spelling test.

Discuss the issue of children not listening or paying attention. Have students give examples of occasions when their children do not pay attention, either in school or at home. Ask students whether or not they need to repeat instructions to their children over and over at home. Ask what students or their children can be distracted by.

Have students recall what they liked to do during recess when they were young. Ask them what their children generally do during recess.

For ESL learners, introduce or review other key vocabulary as needed (e.g., *spelling, listen, directions, number, recess, wait, ready, sorry*).

Exercises (pages 66–69)

Underline the Word from the Story Have students make new sentences using the exercise sentences as models. Encourage students to write about something from their own experience, such as an incident during a test or a warning from a teacher.

Who Says That? List other contexts for the expressions. Ask students when their children might say, "I am not ready" (e.g., "My daughter says, 'I am not ready' when I tell her that she needs to leave for school.").

Spelling Practice at Home Have students create new dialogs using the spelling of other vocabulary from the story. Practice expressions that are appropriate when a child spells a word incorrectly (e.g., "Let's try that one again.").

Discuss with a Partner In Topic 2, encourage students to share effective ways of getting their children ready for tests. Compile a list and have students write good ideas in a notebook or create a poster.

Lesson 12: It's Bedtime

Preview

This story addresses themes of bedtime, the amount of sleep children need, resistance to going to bed, family rules, and bedtime on a non-school night.

Discuss the issue of bedtime and whether or not students make their children go to bed at specific times. Discuss what students think are appropriate bedtimes and adequate amounts of sleep for children of different ages. Ask whether bedtimes vary depending upon the ages of their children.

Encourage students to talk about their child's routine before bedtime at home. Ask, "How long does the process of taking a bath, putting on pajamas, brushing teeth, reading a story, etc., take? In what ways do young children, in particular, stall these proceedings? Why don't some children want to go to bed?"

Ask parents about privileges an older child has that a younger one does not.

Discuss how bedtime routines may vary on the weekends. Ask, "How much later are children permitted to stay up?" Discuss other rules that students may have at home for their children (e.g., No candy before dinner. No television before homework is completed. No playing outside before the bedroom is clean.). If students created a list of rules at home in Lesson 9, refer back to that list. Encourage students to compare and discuss their rules.

For ESL learners, introduce or review other key vocabulary as needed (e.g., *hours, bedtime, pajamas, brush, teeth, sleepy, stay up, later, rule, rest, tired, smiles*).

Exercises (pages 72–75)

Complete the Story Have students create stories about their own children, using the cloze story as a model.

Check the Rules Encourage students to describe the rules they have for specific things on the list (e.g., for *telephone*: "My child is not allowed to talk on the telephone for more than 20 minutes. My child is not allowed to call anyone after 9:00. My child is not allowed to talk on the telephone before finishing her homework.").

Time for Bed Have students create new dialogs in which parents enforce home rules. Alternatively, encourage them to create dialogs in which parents relax a rule a little bit. For example, the parent might give in and allow the child to stay up a little later.

Does Your Child Need More Sleep? Discuss other health issues (e.g., diet and exercise) and how children and adults should address those issues. If possible, bring in health brochures on various topics from a doctor's office and discuss the contents.

Discuss with a Partner In Topic 3, discuss ways to provide a relaxing environment for a child getting ready to go to bed.

Lesson 13: Expensive Shoes

Preview

This story addresses themes of shopping for shoes, comparing prices, looking for bargains, children wanting what is popular, and arguing about expenditures.

Have students share experiences about shopping for shoes and clothes with their children. Ask them why this is often difficult. Encourage students to share how conflicts about what to buy are resolved.

Discuss different styles of shoes that are popular among children in primary or secondary school. Ask students, "What do these shoes look like? Do they have a special brand name? Are there other shoes that look similar?"

Discuss budgeting for clothes and shoes. Ask, "What is the maximum amount of money you would spend on a pair of athletic shoes for your child? How often do you need to buy new ones? Do you buy new ones because they are worn out, because they are too small, or because your child wants something more stylish?"

Have students share how peers at school sometimes influence their children in choice of clothing or other possessions and in other types of behavior. Ask, "What other things do your children see that they also want to have?"

Discuss different ways that children react when they are disappointed about something. Introduce new vocabulary as needed (e.g., *sulk, pout*). Ask,

"Does your child jump up and down? Cry? Argue? Does your child always respect your final decisions when you refuse to buy something?"

For ESL learners, introduce or review other key vocabulary as needed (e.g., *shopping center, price tags, points, expensive, shakes, same, kids, on sale, cheaper, spend, growing*).

Exercises (pages 78–81)

What Is the Category? Expand each category by adding more words to the lists. Encourage students to use the words to create new sentences.

An Argument in the Shoe Store Encourage students to create new dialogs based upon experiences they have had shopping with their children. Some students may want to role-play instances when their children talked them into buying something.

Come to Shoe Palace! After listening to the audio and completing the activity, discuss other ways that shoes are advertised. Bring in or have students bring in ads from newspapers and magazines. Discuss radio and TV ads. Ask students about regular prices, sale prices, store hours, location, etc.

Discuss with a Partner In Topic 2, have students recall something that a child really wanted and the reasons why. Ask how they dealt with the situation.

Lesson 14: Crossing the Street

Preview

This story addresses themes of transportation, walking to school, using caution, reading signs, obeying rules, and getting to school safely.

Review methods of transportation and ask students how their children get to school. For students whose children walk to school, ask what major streets they need to cross. Elicit information about which streets have traffic lights, stop signs, crosswalks, or crossing guards.

Review and discuss the meaning of various traffic signs. Have students describe their shapes and colors and tell what the signs say. Students may want to create a poster or brochure of traffic signs that can be shared with their children.

Have students discuss whether or not their children pay attention to or understand various signs.

Ask students how they remind their children to use caution when crossing streets.

For ESL learners, introduce or review other key vocabulary as needed (e.g., *cross, waits, corner, traffic lights, signs, busy, crosswalk, painted, between, crossing guard, whistle, safely*).

Exercises (pages 84–87)

Complete the Sentences Encourage students to create new sentences using the exercise sentences as models (e.g., "Maddy lives in an apartment. My cousin lives in an apartment. My girlfriend lives in an apartment.").

Conversation at the Corner Have students create new dialogs in which they caution someone who could be taking a risk or doing something dangerous. This conversation could take place at a crosswalk, traffic light, or intersection; at a workplace; or even in the home.

Make a List Using an example from the list of dangerous ways, ask students to explain what could happen to a child who went to school that way.

Discuss with a Partner In Topic 2, have students tell or write their opinions of the safety of the streets in their community. Encourage them to consider some of the hazards and what can be done to improve things for pedestrians.

Lesson 15: Absent from School

Preview

This story addresses themes of sickness, reporting an absence from school, giving a child's full name over the phone, missing work, and parental responsibility.

Review common childhood illnesses. Discuss what an *excused absence* is and what are legitimate reasons for missing school.

Ask students what occurs when parents work and a child is sick. Discuss how employers react when calls are made about missing work because of a sick child.

Discuss ways to treat children who are sick with a cold or the flu. Ask students what they do to take care of a sick child and how they can tell whether or not a child needs to see a doctor.

Have students describe the procedure at their child's school for reporting an absence. Ask, "Are calls supposed to be made to the school office? Is a written note expected when a child returns to school?"

For ESL learners, introduce or review other key vocabulary as needed (e.g., *fever, rest, calls, attendance clerk, absent, grade, stay home, explains, better, still, take care*).

Exercises (pages 90–93)

What Is the Category? Have students expand the categories by adding more words to each list. Encourage them to use the words to create new sentences. Have students show their understanding by explaining the symptoms for each health problem and describing the jobs of people who work at school.

My Son Is Sick Have students create new dialogs reporting other reasons why a child is absent. Encourage students to use their children's names and grade levels for practice. Have them add details that would be needed if they called the child's school, such as the child's room number or the teacher's name.

A Message from the School Have students share reactions to this message. Ask, "What is the first thing this parent needs to do?" Have students practice returning this phone call to the attendance clerk.

Discuss with a Partner In Topic 1, have students talk or write about an occasion when a child was absent for a reason other than illness. Have students evaluate whether it is a good reason to miss school or not. Ask how they explained the reason to the school office.

Level 2 Lesson Notes

Lesson 1: He Can't Be Late

Preview

This story addresses themes of morning routines, being late for school, and a call from the principal.

Encourage students to share what their children typically do in the morning. Ask questions about things that can distract a child getting ready for school. Have students tell whether or not their children usually pay attention to the time.

Elicit names of television cartoons. Ask students if they know what these cartoons are about. Have students discuss whether or not these programs are popular with their children and why.

Discuss tardiness and how seriously it is taken in elementary school and in the upper grades. Ask students why being tardy is considered a serious problem. Discuss whether tardy students go directly to class or report to the school office first. Ask at what point parents are notified about a child's tardiness.

Discuss occasions when a parent might receive a telephone call from the principal. Ask students if they have ever gotten calls from their children's principals. If so, ask students if they would mind telling what the calls were for and how they reacted.

For ESL learners, introduce or review other key vocabulary as needed (e.g., *almost, bowl, cartoons, hear, late, tardy, serious, disruptive, repeat, adult, happen*).

Exercises (pages 6–9)

Make a List After students list reasons children lose track of time, have them share their reasons and discuss their solutions to the problems (e.g., "If my daughter is watching television, I turn it off. If my son is reading the newspaper, I tell him that he can read it later.").

You're Often Late Have students create new dialogs between a parent and child about concerns a teacher or a principal might have (e.g., a child not paying attention in class).

Late for School Have students practice giving new messages about a child's tardiness to the school office. Have the class decide if a message is clear and complete and whether or not the reason for tardiness is acceptable.

Topics for Discussion or Writing In Topic 1, discuss or have students write about the significance of their children being late for other activities (e.g., appointments, extracurricular activities).

Lesson 2: My Head Itches

Preview

This story addresses themes of health, the transmission of head lice, parent notification, and treatment of head lice.

Have students discuss the issue of head lice. Ask if any of their children ever had lice, and if so, ask how the children got them. Ask students how they discovered the problem, what their reaction was, and how they treated it. Students should know that a health issue such as lice can cause embarrassment. However, this is a common problem.

Explore with students the role of a nurse or health aide at school. Have students discuss notices they have received from a child's school about a health concern. Have students describe what the health issue was and whether it was something contagious or transmittable. Elicit their responses to these notices or warnings.

Discuss where to buy shampoo and other necessary items for the treatment of head lice. If students have experience with head lice, ask them to explain additional measures they took (e.g., house-cleaning, washing sheets in hot water, etc.) to get rid of the lice.

For ESL learners, introduce or review other key vocabulary as needed (e.g., *scratching, think, itches, nurse, hair, lice, nits, immediately, special, fine-tooth comb, share, contact, unpleasant, common*).

Exercises (pages 12–15)

Complete the Story After students complete the cloze story, ask questions to check comprehension.

Encourage students to retell the story in their own words.

Finding Head Lice Have students create new dialogs with symptoms of other health problems.

A Letter to Parents Collect or have students bring in other examples of health warnings from a school nurse or health aide. Discuss other contagious illnesses such as chicken pox and strep throat. Discuss which illnesses are the most serious. Have students share ideas on what can be done to prevent a child from spreading or catching an illness at school.

Lesson 3: She Wants to Be Friends

Preview

This story addresses themes of nationality, customs of dress, socializing at school, lunch foods, and making friends.

Find Somalia on a map and elicit or point out the most common languages spoken there: Somali and Arabic. Ask students whether or not they are fluent in a language other than English.

Discuss traditional customs of dress, especially in places where typical clothing differs from western styles. Talk about the type of clothing typically worn by school-age children in your community. Encourage students to share photos of their children, draw pictures, or cut pictures of schoolchildren out of magazines and discuss items of clothing.

Have students tell about the kind of foods their children bring or buy for lunch at school. Discuss what foods children commonly bring or buy for lunch at school in the U.S.

Discuss shyness and whether or not students or their children have ever felt excluded at school. Elicit ideas that students have come up with to help their children feel included.

For ESL learners, introduce or review other key vocabulary as needed (e.g., *native language, fluent, wear, quiet, container, eye contact, probably, shy, alone, idea, game*).

Exercises (pages 18–21)

Which Category Is It? Have students add more items in each category. In the Countries category,

elicit names of the continents where the countries are located. Find the countries on a world map or globe.

Make a List After students complete this activity, encourage them to list qualities they notice about a partner. Have partners share these observations with each other. This can also be done in a small group. In particular, students can describe what a partner (or a volunteer standing in front of the class) is wearing.

What Are These Children Wearing? If students have brought in or drawn pictures of school-age children as part of the Preview, have them write about what the children in those pictures are wearing or ask them to label the items of clothing in the pictures.

Topics for Discussion or Writing For Topic 3, encourage students to bring in a ball, a jump-rope, or another item from a favorite childhood game. Have students explain how each game is played, drawing diagrams or pictures to help clarify their explanation. If possible, have them demonstrate playing this game with another student.

Lesson 4: Don't Throw Away Your Food

Preview

This story addresses themes of school lunches, following cafeteria rules, emotions, wasting food, and identifying a problem that needs to be solved.

Ask students about their children's eating habits. Ask if the children generally eat a lot or a little, and what foods the children like or do not like. Have students share what they do when a child does not finish his or her food at home. Ask if parents know whether or not their children finish their lunches at school.

Encourage students to share information about the cafeterias at their children's schools. Ask if their children comment on whether the food is good or bad and whether there is too much food or not enough. Discuss whether or not children can select from a variety of foods.

Elicit cafeteria rules (e.g., You must throw away your trash; you must carry your tray with two hands; you must not yell indoors.). Have students create a poster listing cafeteria rules.

Discuss the issue of food shortages in the U.S. and in other countries. If students feel comfortable sharing personal information with each other, ask if they or family members have ever experienced not having enough to eat. Discuss how they feel when they see someone throw away food.

For ESL learners, introduce or review other key vocabulary as needed (e.g., *standing, lunchtime, reminds, rules, taking cuts, throw away, garbage cans, full, hungry, native country, enough, anymore*).

Exercises (pages 24–27)

Complete the Story After students complete the story, ask questions to check comprehension. Have students comment on whether Cora should go back to her seat and finish her lunch, or whether she should be allowed to go outside and play.

Planning for Lunch Have students create new dialogs based on an actual school menu, if possible, or on the example on the next page in their book. Discuss whether the meals look appealing or unappealing and why. Have them give examples of lunches their children would prefer.

What's for Lunch? Compare this menu with actual school lunch menus that you provide or have students bring in. (These menus can be found on school web sites). Discuss which schools offer the best selection of food.

Topics for Discussion or Writing For Topic 3, have students research agencies in your area that take food donations. Have students describe or write about the process of donating to these agencies. Discuss which foods would make good donations. Ask why some foods might not make good donations. Discuss how foods are distributed to people in need.

Lesson 5:
A Contract with the Teacher

Preview

This story addresses themes of a parent talking to the teacher, an extended absence, commitment to a school contract, and student accountability.

Ask students if they visited faraway relatives or took trips when they were children. Ask if these visits ever occurred during the school year; if so, ask how long the visit was and what they were expected to do during their absence. Ask students if they had to sign contracts promising that schoolwork would be completed.

Discuss the advantages and disadvantages of traveling during the school year. Elicit students' ideas on what other things, in addition to classwork, a child misses when he or she is absent for a long time.

Have students share opinions about acceptable reasons for children to miss school. Discuss the maximum length of time that students would allow their children to miss school.

Ask students to share strategies for getting schoolwork completed if a child is away from home. Have them consider what time of day is the most productive for their child and when it is convenient to assist the child with schoolwork.

For ESL learners, introduce or review other key vocabulary as needed (e.g., *heart surgery, absent, sign, contract, promises, make sure, returns, checks, assignments, better, finished*).

Exercises (pages 30–33)

Which Category Is It? After students list items in each category, encourage them to give specific examples of schoolwork their child has had (e.g., "My daughter is working on a science project about electricity. My son did a report about the Civil War. My daughter had a math assignment that was very difficult for her.").

What Happened First? Have a student share a story about a time when his or her family went away. Encourage the student to include details about where he or she was going and why. Have other students retell the story, putting at least seven events in order.

Looking at Schoolwork Encourage students to create new dialogs based on a typical exchange with a child about a school assignment. The child can be either cooperative or reluctant to show the homework to the parent.

Ana's Book Report Elicit ideas from students to help Ana improve this book report. Give examples of ways to be clearer or give more details in answering the questions. If possible, have students do a sample book report on a book they have read.

Lesson 6: The Field Trip

Preview

This story addresses themes of volunteering, watching a group of children, going to the zoo, and losing track of a child.

Ask students about places their children have been on school field trips. Have students discuss duties of parent volunteers on a field trip.

Ask students about the zoo in your community or another zoo they are familiar with, perhaps from childhood. Have students describe the zoo, including whether it is large or small, what kind of animals it has, and how much it costs to get in.

Have students share experiences of losing track of a child in a public place. Ask where it happened and how the child was found. Have them discuss what they have taught their child about safety in public places. Discuss strategies for finding a lost child.

For ESL learners, introduce or review key vocabulary as needed (e.g., *field trip, volunteer, noisy, excited, zoo, worried, heart, beating, group, boring, interesting*).

Exercises (pages 36–39)

What Happened First? After students complete the sequencing activity, have a student tell about an experience where he or she helped out on a field trip. On the board, write approximately seven main events from the story in random order. Have students put the events in order.

Reporting a Lost Child Have students create new dialogs using a description of their own children or of a student in the class. Ask them to clarify the setting (e.g., a beach, a department store, a stadium) and tell who they are talking to (e.g., a lifeguard, a sales clerk, an usher).

Class Field Trip After students read the letter and answer the questions, discuss reasons why they would or would not like to volunteer on this field trip. Discuss concerns that some parents might

have about their children going on field trips in general. Raise issues of cost, transportation, supervision, safety, etc.

Topics for Discussion or Writing In Topic 2, have students give strategies for specific locations as well as general suggestions for locating lost children.

Lesson 7: The Report Card

Preview

This story addresses themes of receiving a report card, difficulty understanding a report card, and identifying a problem that needs to be solved.

Elicit from students how often they receive their children's report cards. Ask if report cards are mailed, received at a conference, or hand-delivered by the child.

Provide or have students bring in samples of report cards. Discuss what the letter or number grades mean, and read any accompanying explanation. To help with understanding, provide a filled-in sample or help students fill out blank report cards. Clarify the different subjects or behaviors for which students receive grades or comments.

Discuss the different native languages spoken at children's schools. Ask students whether or not translators are provided or other services are offered to assist parents or children who do not speak English.

Tell students about a time when you needed help in reading or understanding something from a school. Tell who you asked for help (e.g., a family member, a neighbor, or your child). Describe how that person was or was not helpful.

For ESL learners, introduce or review other key vocabulary as needed (e.g., *unlock, mailbox, envelope, report card, comments, dictionary, conference, translator, neighbor, personal*).

Exercises (pages 42–45)

Complete the Story After students complete the cloze story, ask questions to check comprehension. Ask students to share their experiences at parent-teacher conferences.

Talking about a Report Card Have students create new dialogs about other marks or symbols that might cause confusion (e.g., "What does the check mark mean? What does the zero mean? What does the dash mean?").

Sonya's Report Card Create additional comments typically found on report cards and share them with the students. Decide which comments are favorable and which are unfavorable.

Topics for Discussion or Writing In Topic 3, encourage students to discuss or write about a time when they disagreed with a child's report card. Have them identify what they did not agree with and why. Ask if they discussed their opinions with the teachers, and if so, whether anything changed as a result.

Lesson 8: After-School Care

Preview

This story addresses themes of after-school routines, working parents, and after-school child care.

Ask students when their children's school day is over. Have students discuss what their children do immediately after school. Ask, for example, if the child goes directly home or stays in an after-school program. If the latter, ask what the name of the program is and what the child does there.

Share observations about activities that commonly occur in before- and after-school care programs. Discuss how many staff members usually supervise these programs. Have students tell how early in the morning or how late in the evening children may be in the programs.

Encourage students to discuss reasons why parents use these services. Discuss why some parents have concerns about their child being home alone. Have students share opinions on the advantages and disadvantages of these programs.

For ESL learners, introduce or review other key vocabulary as needed (e.g., *over, care, alone, adults, playground, ball, homework, finish, pick up, ready*).

Exercises (pages 48–51)

Write Some Reasons After completing this activity, encourage students to share positive and negative experiences they had with a before- or after-school program (e.g., "The staff at the after-school care program seemed to care about the kids a lot. My daughter didn't enjoy the before-school care at all. She didn't get along very well with the other children.").

Staying Late Have students create new dialogs about when and why a parent may be late picking up a child. Mention fees or other consequences a parent might face.

Topics for Discussion or Writing In Topic 1, have students discuss or write about personal feelings they have about a child being home alone. Raise issues of trust, maturity, safety, etc.

Lesson 9: Hurt Feelings at School

Preview

This story addresses themes of emotions, parental concern, harassment at school, and reporting unpleasant incidents to the school.

Ask students about signs that may indicate when something is bothering a child. Discuss changes in appetite, behavior, emotions, etc. Talk about ways of reassuring children who are having problems with others at school.

Discuss ways that boys and girls tease, taunt, or harass each other. Raise the issue of name-calling or making fun of someone. Ask students whether making fun of someone is serious or not, and why. Have students share personal experiences they have had in dealing with these issues.

Elicit responses from students about problems that are serious enough to report to a child's school. Have students name people to contact about specific problems (e.g., teacher, principal, counselor, other parents, the police, etc.).

For ESL learners, introduce or review other key vocabulary as needed (e.g., *snack, straight, crying, knocks, floor, shoulder, teasing, make fun, hurt feelings, miserable, furious, rule, respect, worse*).

Exercises (pages 54–57)

Which Category Is It? If possible, have students list more items in each category. For the Emotions category, encourage students to talk about what might cause the emotions listed.

Reporting a Problem Have students create new dialogs about infractions of other school rules. Encourage students to give specific details with their complaints.

Check the Behaviors Have students suggest ways that children can respond to each of the mean behaviors, and evaluate which responses are effective ways of dealing with the problems.

Lesson 10:
He Can't Do Multiplication

Preview

This story addresses themes of homework, difficulties doing multiplication, parental support, and problem solving.

Encourage students to talk about various homework assignments for children. In particular, discuss whether children have to practice arithmetic skills at home and if so, which ones (addition, subtraction, multiplication, division, etc.).

Have students recall how they learned to multiply numbers. Discuss methods of memorization, e.g., using tables or flash cards. Elicit descriptions of the way multiplication is taught in schools today.

Have students write examples of multiplication problems, showing different ways of indicating the multiplication function. Have students from other countries demonstrate how multiplication problems are written in their countries. Make sure they are familiar with how math problems are written in this country.

Have students describe instances when an assignment caused their children to become frustrated. Ask students to share methods they have used at home to help their children understand math concepts. If appropriate, mention stores in the community or other sources (like libraries) where parents can find instructional materials to use to help their children.

For ESL learners, introduce or review other key vocabulary as needed (e.g., *assignment, correct, answers, multiplication, counts, fingers, remember, times (×), memorize, flash cards, practice, agrees*).

Exercises (pages 60–63)

Complete the Story After students complete the cloze story, ask questions to check comprehension. Encourage students to retell this story in their own words or to write a story using another math operation, such as subtraction or division.

Practicing Multiplication Have students create new dialogs using other multiplication problems. They may also wish to role-play practicing addition, substituting the word *plus* for *times,* and then solving the problems.

Parent-Teacher Conference After students listen to the comments and answer the questions, have them think of other ways to reassure Alisha and to help her prepare for the next timed addition test.

Topics for Discussion or Writing In Topic 1, encourage students to share challenges they had or continue to have with a particular subject. In a whole-class or small-group activity, discuss or write about ways to strengthen a child's confidence and skills.

Lesson 11: She Talks Too Much

Preview

This story addresses themes of popularity, talking in class, changing seats, and annoying the teacher.

Elicit from students a list of behaviors that can be disruptive in class (e.g., talking, leaving one's seat without permission, tardiness, etc.). In particular, discuss talking at inappropriate times and how that affects other students and the teacher.

Have students share stories about themselves when they were schoolchildren. Ask if they were friendly and outgoing or more shy and reserved. Ask if they had any behavior problems that occasionally got them in trouble, and if so, what those problems were.

Discuss discipline strategies that a teacher might use to combat talking or other behavior problems in class. Ask students what their children's teachers do to discipline students.

For ESL learners, introduce or review other key vocabulary as needed (e.g., *popular, smart, problem, behave, seat, quietest, minutes, repeat, appreciate, sorry, anymore, chance, alone*).

Exercises (pages 66–69)

What Happened First? After students complete the sequencing activity, have a student tell about an experience when he or she got into trouble with the teacher. On the board, write approximately seven main events from the story in random order. Have students put the events in order and retell the story.

You Aren't Listening Have students create new dialogs with infractions of other class rules. Encourage students who play the teacher's role to take appropriate disciplinary action.

A Note from the Teacher Have students imagine that they received this note about their child. Ask how they would react and what they would say to the child. Ask if there would be punishment or other consequences at home.

Topics for Discussion or Writing In Topic 2, encourage students to share ideas about effective solutions to the problems they discuss or write about.

Lesson 12: Invitation to a Friend's House

Preview

This story addresses themes of friendship, responding to an invitation, parental concern, and family rules.

Discuss friendship. Have students talk about friends they had while growing up. Encourage them to talk about whether they played with friends outside of school, where they played, and whether a parent was present if they were at home.

Ask students whether or not their children have ever received invitations to play at a friend's house, attend a birthday party, or spend the night with a friend. If so, ask how they react to these invitations and what they do when they do not know the other child's parents or do not live in the same community. Encourage them to discuss why they would or would not allow their children to go to a friend's house to play, attend a party, sleep over, or take part in some other activity. Discuss rules in students' families about socializing outside of school.

Have students share concerns they have about their children visiting the homes of people they do not know. Discuss the pros and cons of allowing such visits.

For ESL learners, introduce or review other key vocabulary as needed (e.g., *get along, together, excited, invitation, computer games, uncomfortable, watch, neighborhood, safe, enough, rule, happen, disappoint*).

Exercises (pages 72–75)

Which Category Is It? If possible, have students list more items in each category. Ask students if they have pets now, or if they had pets as children. Who took care of the animals?

Write Some Reasons Ask students if there are ever exceptions to any of their rules and the conditions for an exception (e.g., "My child is not allowed to spend the night at a friend's house, but I might consider allowing it once I visit the home and meet the parents.").

Questions and Answers Create new question-and-answer dialogs beginning with a child's request to do something or go somewhere with another child at school. Encourage students to express the concerns they would normally have in similar situations.

A Message from Mrs. Anderson After students listen to the message and answer the questions, encourage them to share any concerns they would still have after hearing Kathleen's message.

Topics for Discussion or Writing In Topic 3, have students talk or write about a time when they declined an invitation. Encourage them to specify whether they declined in person, in a note, or on the telephone, and to tell exactly what they said. Students may wish to create dialogs or role-plays based on these situations.

Lesson 13: The School Dress Code

Preview

This story addresses themes of a school dress code, parental cooperation, peer pressure, fashion, and the desire to express one's individuality.

Have students discuss school dress codes and

describe the policies at their children's schools. Have them tell if there are specific styles and colors that must be worn, and if so, to describe them. Encourage students to express their opinions about whether or not a dress code or school uniform is a good policy, and if it is easier or cheaper, and why. Discuss benefits and drawbacks of having a student dress code.

Elicit descriptions from students of the clothing that their children wear to school. Have them describe clothing they would not allow a child to wear to school.

Have students describe instances when their child wanted something that another child had (clothing, toys, privileges, etc.). Ask how they responded to the child, including what they said to resolve the issue.

For ESL learners, introduce or review key vocabulary as needed (e.g., *follow, dress code, skirt, pants, closet, voluntary, colorful, stylish, boring*).

Exercises (pages 78–81)

Complete the Story After students complete the cloze story, ask questions to check comprehension. Encourage students to rewrite this story using details about their children's schools and different characters (one of whom might be their child).

Looking for School Clothes Have students create new dialogs based on conversations about clothing with their children (e.g., "Is a T-shirt okay? Yes, it is, as long as it has the school logo."). They may also create dialogs between parents and children in a clothing store.

On Sale Provide or have students bring in newspaper advertisements featuring children's clothing. Check understanding of promotions and clothing items noted in the ads. Discuss which stores offer the best prices.

Topics for Discussion or Writing In Topic 1, encourage students to talk or write about why a dress code may be helpful to children. Raise issues of blending in and focusing on learning instead of on fashion. Alternatively, have students talk or write about reasons why a school dress code may be harmful to children. If appropriate, students can hold a debate on the topic.

Lesson 14: Playground Safety

Preview

This story addresses themes of playing at recess, weather-appropriate clothing, disobeying school rules, and getting hurt at school.

Elicit responses from students about how much time their children have for recess. Ask what games or activities their children generally engage in at recess. Discuss whether children play inside or outside when the weather is bad. Ask about the surface on which the children play (e.g., grass, sand, blacktop) and whether it is safe for children.

Have students share common playground safety rules from their children's schools. Encourage them to think about common injuries children may suffer while playing and how to prevent those injuries. Ask students if there are rules about activities children cannot do on playgrounds. Ask if they think those rules are a good idea or not.

Encourage students to share incidents where their children got hurt at school. Ask how the child got hurt, whether the child went to the school nurse, and if so, what the nurse did.

Review clothing vocabulary if necessary, particularly the names of clothing and accessories worn in the winter. Ask students what their children wear to school when the weather is cold, rainy, snowy, etc.

Discuss the role of an adult on playground duty. Ask students if this job is usually performed by a teacher, the principal, or a parent volunteer. Ask students if they have ever supervised children during playtime, and if so, whether it was necessary to tend to any children with minor injuries.

For ESL learners, introduce or review other key vocabulary as needed (e.g., *recess, playing, jumping rope, jacket, hurry, running, blacktop, dangerous*).

Exercises (pages 84–87)

What Happened First? After students complete the sequencing activity, have a student tell about an experience when his or her child was injured at school. On the board, write approximately seven main events from the story at random. Have students put the events in order.

Reporting an Injury Have students create new dialogs reporting other common childhood injuries, giving reasons for the injuries. Review vocabulary for body parts if necessary.

How Did These Children Get Hurt? For each picture, have students describe what could be done to prevent each injury. Discuss playground safety rules that may have been violated.

Topics for Discussion or Writing In Topic 2, encourage students to tell or write about the area where their children play at school. Have students consider the safety of playground equipment. Ask about supervision of the play area. Encourage students to tell what things they would change if they could.

Lesson 15: She's Always Absent

Preview

This story addresses themes of unexcused absences, reasons that a child misses school, the negative effects of chronic absences, responses and concerns of school personnel, and the importance of education.

Ask students the approximate number of school days their children miss in a school year. Have them identify typical reasons for these absences. As a class, distinguish excused and unexcused absences.

Have students explain the responsibilities their children have at home. Discuss activities like cleaning or babysitting. With students from non-English-speaking backgrounds, ask if children ever act as interpreters for family members, and if so, when and where they perform these duties.

Ask students about the effects of missing school. Have them consider what happens when a child returns to school and how well the child understands what is going on in class. Ask about the short-term and long-term consequences of missing a lot of school. Discuss when they feel a teacher or principal should get involved if a child is absent a lot.

For ESL learners, introduce or review other key vocabulary as needed (e.g., *healthy, translates, absent/absence, unexcused, acceptable, confused, concerned*).

Exercises (pages 90–93)

Write Some Reasons After students list and evaluate reasons that children may be absent from school, encourage them to consider ways to reduce absences, even for acceptable reasons.

Parents Discussing an Absence Create new dialogs about other reasons for an excused absence. Encourage students to tell about instances when their children were absent and they forgot to notify the school. Have them tell what happened as a result.

My Son Is Absent Have students practice writing notes excusing their children from school. Use the example as a model. Make sure students are specific about the child's name, the dates, the teacher's name, and the reason for the absence.

Topics for Discussion or Writing In Topic 3, encourage students to talk or write about practical ways to support a child who must miss school for a long period of time. Students may want to refer to Lesson 5. Have them consider strategies like regular communication with the teacher, helping the child keep up with class work, using the services of a tutor, etc.